HISTORIC PHOTOS OF
PALM BEACH
COUNTY

TEXT AND CAPTIONS BY SETH H. BRAMSON

TURNER
PUBLISHING COMPANY
NASHVILLE, TENNESSEE   PADUCAH, KENTUCKY

With Florida's then-ubiquitous coconut palms waving in the breeze, photographer Charles Barron presented downtown West Palm Beach across Lake Worth early in 1960.

HISTORIC PHOTOS OF
PALM BEACH
COUNTY

Turner Publishing Company

200 4th Avenue North • Suite 950   412 Broadway • P.O. Box 3101
Nashville, Tennessee 37219   Paducah, Kentucky 42002-3101
(615) 255-2665   (270) 443-0121

www.turnerpublishing.com

Historic Photos of Palm Beach County

Library of Congress Control Number: 2007929607

ISBN-13: 978-1-59652-402-6

Printed in the United States of America

07 08 09 10 11 12 13 14—0 9 8 7 6 5 4 3 2 1

CONTENTS

In 1898, the Chicago-based Little Chronicle Publishing Company produced a fine stereoscopic card showing one of the numerous pedicabs known as "Afromobiles" that would, by the Teens and 1920s, become ubiquitous in Palm Beach. A black driver pedaled passengers around town as they relaxed in their moving lounge chair.

ACKNOWLEDGMENTS

This volume, *Historic Photos of Palm Beach County,* is the result of the cooperation and efforts of many individuals, organizations, and corporations. It is with great thanks that we acknowledge the valuable contribution of the following for their generous support:

Collection of Seth H. Bramson
Library of Congress
State Archives of Florida

PREFACE

When one thinks of, speaks about, or writes the history of Palm Beach County, an appropriate reference is that wonderful line from the 1960s, "What a trip." For the history of Palm Beach County is, at be very least, a true "trip," in the ethereal—and certainly in the historical—sense.

Palm Beach became its own county in 1909 but prior to that was part of what was then a much-larger Dade County. In fact, from 1889 until 1899—when the population of southern Dade County became large enough to return the county seat to the shores of Biscayne Bay—Juno, at the far north end of what was then Dade County (now Palm Beach County) was the county seat.

Nowhere else in America was there a "Celestial Railroad." The 7.5-mile Jupiter and Lake Worth Railroad running through Jupiter, Juno, Venus, and Mars opened in 1889. Oil magnate and railroad developer Henry Morrison Flagler put it out of business when he brought his own rail line into West Palm Beach five years later. He erected a home now considered one of the ten most magnificent private homes in America and built two of the most glorious winter resorts in the nation.

Palm Beach County today is certainly more than "just" West Palm Beach or Palm Beach, although the former remains the county seat. It boasts innumerable first-class clubs and residential developments, beautifully maintained private homes, world-class tourist destinations, and numerous museums, art galleries, auditoriums, and concert venues. Home to the fastest-growing Jewish community in America, its population is nearing one-and-a-half million people.

From Boca Raton and the Boca Raton Club on the south to Jupiter, Loxahatchee, and the PGA club and course in the north, Palm Beach County, with its fabled history, is a highly desirable destination for any Floridaphile, writer, or historian. The images on these pages capture the fascinating story of the county in a unique presentation.

With the exception of touching up imperfections caused by the vicissitudes of time and cropping where necessary, no other changes have been made to the photographs in this book. The focus and clarity of many images is limited to the technology of the day and the skill of the photographer who captured them. Many will spark warm, personal memories for readers, while others provide a glimpse into an era long gone—when Florida East Coast Railway trains crossed Lake Worth to serve the super-rich "resorting" at the Breakers and the Royal Poinciana and a mule car operated between the two hotels, until the great 1925 fire destroyed the second Breakers. Palm Beach County is one of the most recognizable names and locations in the world. These are images of the people, places, buildings and events that made it so.

Shown on March 19, 1930, the venerable Royal Poinciana is nearly empty, made obsolete by newer, more modern, "fireproof" hotels, complete with amenities not even dreamed of when the RP was built. Sadly, the hotel would last only one more season, when it was ignominiously dismantled. Its furnishing and fixtures were sold for pennies on the dollar to any and all who had the money to buy them. Although the Breakers, the P. B. Biltmore, the Whitehall, and other properties would soldier on, the loss of the Poinciana was, in many ways, a bellwether of the changes being thrust upon Palm Beach.

Little More Than a Wilderness Till '94

(1889–1899)

There was rejoicing in the north end of Dade County in 1889. It had a larger population than the southern section of the sparsely inhabited county, which allowed it to win an election, replacing Biscayne (later called Miami) with Juno as the county seat. The euphoria would not last long. By 1899, population demographics had shifted, and the seat of government moved back to its former location. The northern part of the county would neither accept it nor "get over it," and the unhappiness lasted until Palm Beach was able to form its own county ten years later.

In the meantime, the "Barefoot Mailman" (memorialized in Theodore Pratt's fine book of the same name) became a collective term for mail carriers on the Palm Beach–Miami route who traveled by boat and by walking barefoot along the beach. The Celestial Railroad (officially the Jupiter and Lake Worth Railway) and announcements by the Flagler interests that they would build two hotels on Palm Beach and extend the Jacksonville, St. Augustine, and Indian River Railway to the shores of Lake Worth generated great excitement. In May 1893, ground was broken for the Royal Poinciana Hotel, and with great fanfare the building opened in February 1894. One month later, on March 22, the railroad arrived at West Palm Beach.

The great freezes of December 1894 and January-February 1895 destroyed truck (produce) and citrus crops along nearly the entire length of Florida, abating south of the New River. Julia Tuttle, who had become the only woman ever to establish a U.S. city when she developed Miami, convinced Flagler to extend his railroad to Biscayne Bay by showing him that fruit had survived further south and by giving him half of her land north of the river, with 50 additional acres for shops and yards. William Brickell donated half of his land south of the river, and surveying for the railway extension south from West Palm Beach began in June 1895. Later that summer, the Flagler Hotel Company announced construction of a second Palm Beach property, the Palm Beach Inn, later to be known as The Breakers. On September 8, 1895, the railroad was rechristened the Florida East Coast (FEC) Railway, the name it retains today. The Palm Beach Inn opened in January 1896. The two hotels and the railroad drew to the town of Palm Beach the grandest, wealthiest, most elegant segments of society. Their influence would spread throughout much of the county.

What appears to be a picture of two trains at Palm Beach is actually a rare photograph showing an FEC steam passenger train on the south track with the old Breakers in the background and the FEC's mule car to the right. Henry Flagler built Whitehall as a wedding gift to his bride, but she complained about the noise of the trains coming across Lake Worth, so he had the bridge pulled up and moved north of the mansion. The south track remained in use only for the mule car, which shuttled back and forth across the island.

From its earliest years, Palm Beach was a boating haven. In this 1891 view from the Louise Frisbee collection, at least five sailboats are visible at the Coconut Grove House dock. The Frisbee collection is and was a major resource of early Palm Beach photos and images.

Although diminished because of shrinking schools and changing tourist interests, fishing remains a major draw on the southeast Florida coast. One of the earliest known photographs of the sport in the Palm Beach area—taken March 18, 1893—shows a group posing with their catch of the day, a huge hammerhead shark. They most likely were tourists.

What would become the Coconut Grove House was originally the home of Mr. and Mrs. E. N. Dimick, one of the earliest of the Palm Beach homes opened for guests. This 1891 view shows a group of visitors and at least one servant posing at the rear of the property.

Henry Flagler's magnificent Royal Poinciana Hotel was the first of his two Palm Beach hostelries, opening in early 1894. During construction, toward the end of 1893, a group of plumbers and other tradesmen posed for a photograph on the lawn of the unfinished edifice.

This 1895 image from the Frisbee collection is believed to show a westward-facing view of an area then known as "the Styx," where today's Sunrise Avenue meets County Road in Palm Beach.

In 1893, three years before Miami incorporated, West Palm Beach was already engaging in cultural events. A group from the Mangonia schoolhouse in the northwest section of the city put on a live performance that year of a play titled "Streets of Cairo" and, fortunately for posterity, posed in costume for this photograph.

In 1895, with Lake Worth, the ferry dock, the FEC bridge, and the Royal Poinciana Hotel in the background, Mr. and Mrs. Louis Burkhardt and their four children pose for the photographer at their lakefront home site at the foot of what is today's Fern Street. This property later became the site of the Lake Court Hotel.

A winsome young Turalura Lipschitz was completely in vogue for a day at the beach on March 21, 1895, her outfit complete with the de rigueur leg coverings of the day and her bathing suit made of wool.

By 1896, Flagler and others had already begun to include parks in their planning for both Palm Beach and West Palm Beach. In this view taken that year, a group of vacationers— appropriately dressed for the era—is enjoying the tropical South Florida winter weather.

For the younger set, a trip to Palm Beach in the winter invariably included the opportunity to enjoy bicycling throughout the island. With the Breakers in the background, this lad is enjoying his riding time during the 1896–97 winter season while his parents were likely at the pool or having lunch at one of the Flagler hotel dining spots.

By the late 1890s, bathing had become a popular Palm Beach pastime. The "Bathing Pavilion" on the Atlantic Ocean beach opposite Lake Worth was a popular rendezvous for the young and adventuresome of the time.

Before Mr. Flagler began his steamship service from Miami to Key West and Nassau, a long pier, complete with rail connection, was built into the ocean at Palm Beach to accommodate coastal steamers. The pier lasted into the early twentieth century, though in its later years it was devoid of tracks and steamboats. In this 1896 view a group of Palm Beach "resorters" is enjoying the surf and sand just south of the pier.

On March 14, 1896, in one of the most famous Palm Beach photos ever taken, a group of very wealthy American tourists posed in front of an FEC passenger train and the Royal Poinciana hotel. From left to right are Col. Philip M. Lydig, Helen Morton, Gladys Vanderbilt, Amy Townsend, Capt. A. T. Rose, Mrs. Cornelius Vanderbilt, Edith Bishop, Mabel Gerry, Thomas Cushing, Edward Livingston, Dudley Winthrop, Craig Wadsworth, Gertrude Vanderbilt, Lispenard Stewart, Harry P. Whitney, Sybil Sherman and Cornelius Vanderbilt.

The legendary Henry M. Flagler would spend $2 million in 1901–1902 dollars to build Whitehall, shown here shortly after completion. Today, it is considered one of America's ten most magnificent private homes and houses the Henry M. Flagler Museum.

Complete with sun parasol, Tondalaya Lipschitz (the twin sister of Turalura, shown on page 10), does her part in beautifying the Palm Beach scene as she poses in her lovely white beach outfit in 1896.

This image, from a late 1890s Little Chronicle stereocard, captures the loveliness of the island of Palm Beach, with its Australian Pine Walkway between the two Flagler hotels, connecting the east (Atlantic Ocean) side and west (Lake Worth) side of the island.

THE ERA OF MR. FLAGLER

(1900–1909)

The cities and towns of northern Dade County began their meteoric growth in the first years of the twentieth century. Florida East Coast Railway advertising showed winter-weary souls up north an image of a cloud-enshrouded globe with the sun shining brightly on Florida, assuring them, "The east coast of Florida is paradise regained."

When the owners of the Celestial Railroad would not sell to Flagler, he simply built his own railroad to the west and named the station West Jupiter, then refused to connect with the Jupiter and Lake Worth Railway. With no interchange of any kind, the J&LW withered and soon died. The FEC's passenger timetable number 30, dated January 28, 1901, shows trains stopped at West Jupiter, Riviera (later Riviera Beach), West Palm Beach, Hotel Royal Poinciana, The Breakers (the Flagler Memorial Bridge connects Palm Beach and West Palm Beach where the FEC's trains once crossed Lake Worth), Lantana, Hypoluxo, Boynton, Delray, and Boca Ratone (the "e" was later removed from the city's name). Lake Worth (the city) was not yet large enough to warrant a passenger station.

During the winter season of 1900–1901, three through trains operated from Jacksonville to Miami, carrying guests to the two Palm Beach hotels from both directions. At the same time, more people, learning about Florida's year-round summerlike weather, began to trickle in to the state. Many lingered in the northern areas of Dade County before moving on to the south, and some of them decided the region from Jupiter to Boca Ratone would be a fine place to farm, build a home, and raise a family.

Still, a large number of people at the northern end of the county were dissatisfied. The county seat once again lay some sixty-five miles to the south. Unhappiness grew concerning taxation, inadequate representation, and other issues stemming from the distance to the seat of government.

Finally in 1909, after years of discussion, the state legislature approved separating over two thousand square miles from Dade County to create a new government entity. The County of Palm Beach was born!

The growth from jungle to village and tourist destination was just a portent of the times to come.

The idea of spending the day fishing in the Gulf Stream enticed innumerable thrill-seekers who kept the charter boat captains busy throughout the winter season. This picture taken around 1900 shows why the charter fishing boat business would increase for years to come.

The pool at the Palm Beach Inn was a busy place, even in 1900. Bathing, whether in surf or pool, was always a delight. The etiquette and protocols of the day forbade anything other than full-body coverings for ladies and modest swimwear for men, but the beaches and pools of Palm Beach County still attracted people of all ages and both genders.

Now located in West Palm Beach, the Gun Club was originally on the Palm Beach side and was yet another of the numerous venues for sports enthusiasts. Shown here around 1900, the interest in the sport is evident from the number of spectators on the second floor balcony as well as on the first floor behind the participants. During this era, almost all entertainment originated at or was connected to the Flagler System hotels.

The *Palm Beach Post* is a respected South Florida newspaper. Originally named the *Daily Lake Worth News*, it became the *Palm Beach Post* in 1916. One of the rarest Florida newspaper photographs that exists, this image from around 1900 of the paper's printing room brings the era of early Florida newspaper publishing to life.

For many children visiting Palm Beach, the greatest single memory was a ride on the FEC's mule-operated trolley car that ran back and forth between the two great Flagler hotels in the winter season. With the second Breakers fire of 1925 the service ended, and when the new Breakers opened a year and a half later, the trolley— the last railroad-operated, animal-powered streetcar in America—was gone, never to be reinstituted, with only some great photographs and fading memories to recall it.

The Royal Poinciana Hotel was the site of lavish entertainments as well as tennis tournaments for men and women—played separately in those days, of course. Here, around 1900, a group of female tennis aficionados enjoy the game while more than a few onlookers enjoy the action.

The Breakers Hotel and the mule car in 1901. Since the track is on the south side of the hotel, the view is northwest and this is the first Breakers, which would be destroyed by fire June 9, 1903, and subsequently rebuilt.

On June 9, 1903, The Breakers hotel was a roaring inferno. The exact cause of the fire, which occurred while the hotel was closed during the summer, was never determined. From the long pier, the view is west and the building on the left, the bathing casino, would be the only part of the property not leveled by or because of the fire.

The Breakers fire is raging and summer beachgoers are witnessing an incredible spectacle as the wooden hotel burns to the ground. Fortunately, because it was not "the season," there were no guests or employees on the property, other than a few caretakers.

In the first decade of the new century, the towns north and south of Palm Beach and West Palm Beach were developing slowly. Here, around 1909, a guest at the Boynton Hotel poses in the requisite attire of the day, complete with necktie. The hotel was a lovely place for those with less formal tastes than the Palm Beach hotels demanded.

"Resorting" from Palm Beach's earliest days had its requisite daily moments, one of those being the post-luncheon choices of bathing, shooting at the Gun Club, golfing on the island's links, tennis, an excursion to the mainland, or, for many, the relaxing pleasure of the social time afforded with friends as guests gathered on the Royal Poinciana porch to greet and gossip while deciding what they would have for dinner.

Then, as now, golf was a delight, at least for those who played the game and not "at the game!" In 1905, both men and women are preparing for tee off, with kibitzers off to the right under the palm tree.

Though bathing pictures of early Palm Beach abound, this one is rare as well as important, for it shows the safety line which could be used by those who were not proficient swimmers. The pier, in the background of this 1904 photo, was no longer used by Flagler System steamboats but had a small windmill in place to show which direction the sea breezes were coming from.

One of northern Dade County's first brick schools, shown shortly after it's opening in 1908, this fine two-story edifice was the central school for the area north of Delray. Children often had to travel long distances in those years to reach a place of learning.

This driver/conductor of the mule car wears an FEC uniform and is accompanied on the platform by a black man, also in uniform, who likely served as porter and groom, walking the mule to the opposite end of the car following each trip.

Breakers and Royal Poinciana guests were fiercely loyal to their chosen hotel, most remaining as guests at one or the other for many seasons. The Breakers porch, shown here around 1905, was to Breakers guests what the RP's verandah was to its aficionados. It became a wonderful gathering spot each day after lunch and sometimes in the evening when events were not planned.

This 1905 image shows a busy day at the beach. One sign tries to draw visitors to Alligator Joe's daily performance. The other, in the center of the picture, bears the words "The bathing hours on this beach are 11 to 1 during which expert life guards and boatmen are provided for the safety of casino guests. Please be guided by their advice when entering the water." The casino referred to is not a gambling casino, but, rather, The Breakers' bathing casino.

The rumblings of discontent with being a part of Dade County were getting louder and the former Dade County Bank, shown here in this Resler Photo Studio view, changed its name to The Pioneer Bank before the 1909 secession from Dade County occurred. It is not known if the bank survived with its new name through the great boom and into the bust of the late 1920s.

From the Louise Frisbee collection comes this photo of a group of African American pedicab drivers waiting for their fares at the Palm Beach FEC depot. A wealthy industrialist's private railroad car is clearly visible in the background.

On July 4, 1908, the local Home Guard marched north on Narcissus Avenue. Wilbur Hendrickson, on horseback, is leading the fire laddies and officers of the then-volunteer fire department. A note says the little girl visible at right would later become Mrs. Dunkle but does not give her first name.

Two New Counties!

(1910–1919)

More and more Americans were learning about and coming to Florida as the decade of the Teens began. The Flagler System hotels, from Atlantic Beach east of Jacksonville to the Royal Palm in Miami, along with the Long Key Fishing Camp in the Florida Keys, were the main destinations.

There was more unrest in south Florida regarding the demarcation of the then-contiguous Palm Beach and Dade counties, and in 1915, the state legislature approved the creation of another county from parts of the existing two. Named "Broward" in honor of former Florida governor Napoleon Bonaparte Broward, it began just north of Ojus in Dade County and extended to the north end of Deerfield Beach in Palm Beach County. With that geographic adjustment, Palm Beach County's existing corporate limits were set.

Miami Beach was not incorporated until 1915; Palm Beach ranked far ahead of it as a resort and tourist destination during this decade, but an era of innocence was about to end. In April 1917, America entered The Great War, then raging in Europe.

Southeast Florida became a training ground for the military, though not on the scale it would see in World War II. The U.S. railroad system, including the Florida East Coast, was taken over by the government in 1918 "for the duration" and the FEC, though retaining its former management, was under federal control until 1920.

Henry Flagler, in his own lifetime, was accorded a god-like reverence. His greatest triumph was building the Key West Extension (the "Oversea Railroad"), a feat of engineering and construction that many at first called "Flagler's Folly," but which came to be referred to as "the eighth wonder of the world." After riding the first train into Key West in 1912, Flagler returned to Whitehall, his Palm Beach mansion. Although suffering from diminished vision and loss of hearing, he remained active as chairman of the Flagler System, which encompassed not just the railway and the hotel company, but numerous South Florida land companies and allied enterprises such as water, gas, and power companies, the FEC Car Ferry Company, the P & O Steamship Company, and several newspapers.

In March 1913, he lost his footing and fell while descending the private staircase under the grand staircase at Whitehall, breaking his hip. On May 20, 1913, Florida's empire builder, a man many consider the greatest person in the history of the Sunshine State, passed away. His death was marked by memorials and obituaries in newspapers throughout the country, but the railroad, his companies and the Palm Beaches he did so much to develop would go on. At decade's end, the county would begin a land boom unprecedented in the state's history.

This 1911 image presents Palm Beach in its transitional stage, still a semi-jungle, but already built up on the Lake Worth and ocean sides. Cutting through the wild areas were paths used by walkers and by the pedicab (later called Afromobile) drivers as they steered their charges through miles of Palm Beach forest, an experience that became a "must" for the affluent in the first two decades of the twentieth century.

The initial manned and powered flight of the Wright Brothers at Kitty Hawk was but eight years in the past when John A. D. McCurdy brought his Curtiss biplane to West Palm Beach in 1911. McCurdy's flights with the first aeroplane (the initial spelling) to visit Palm Beach County were for the purpose of selling land, most likely in cooperation with the early Palm Beach-area land developers Harold Bryant and William Greenwood, who were based in Chicago and were publicizing and selling land under the moniker of the Palm Beach Farms Land Company.

In the early years of the twentieth century, northern Palm Beach County schoolchildren were brought to their places of learning by horse-drawn school buses. Here, in 1911, a group of children of various ages poses with their equine-powered conveyance.

One of the earliest of the West Palm Beach hotels was The Palms, shown here in February 1912 with a horse-drawn wagon in the foreground.

Today, Datura and Dixie in West Palm Beach is a major intersection pulsing with traffic twenty-four hours a day. This photograph, taken prior to 1914, shows a peaceful image of the location, with the original Episcopal Church, made entirely of wood.

It is believed that the first public auction of land in Palm Beach County was held in 1912, only three years after separation from Dade County in 1909. Standing in front of the real estate office and The Bookstore, which was also a Rexall Drug agency, a group of prospective buyers eagerly awaits the start of the auction.

By late 1912, the Florida Coast Line Canal and Transportation Company, partially owned by Henry Flagler, had completed a good portion of what was to become the Atlantic Intracoastal Waterway, with the section from Fort Pierce south to West Palm Beach newly opened. Tours along the coast were usually heavily booked and the fortunate group on board is enjoying a long-gone view of Florida's once scenic and pristine coast line.

One of the symbols of growth for American cities in the early years of the century was a fully funded marching band, which would participate in parades, holiday events, and other worthy happenings. West Palm Beach was no exception, and their twenty-piece ensemble posed proudly for a photographer.

By 1916, a great city was beginning to take shape. A section of the downtown business district, with shoreline still recognizable today, basks in the warm winter sunlight as West Palm began to take on a business and residential character while Palm Beach became the tourist destination and domicile for the very wealthy.

Clematis Street was and remains one of West Palm Beach's primary commercial thoroughfares. This 1916 image shows the influx of automobiles for local transportation, parked in the middle of the street. Clematis has changed so dramatically that none of what is shown here is recognizable today.

In 1916, Clematis Street, as one of West Palm's most important business arteries, was also used for celebratory parades and other events. Thanks to Byron's Photo, this view of the first Seminole Sun Dance was made and preserved.

Henry Flagler, in addition to his great commercial ventures, funded numerous churches along the east coast of Florida. In 1895, he provided the money to build the Royal Poinciana Chapel, also known as the Flagler Church and later as the Little White Chapel. Originally built on the grounds of the Royal Poinciana Hotel, it was later moved to Coconut Row in Palm Beach.

Growth brought expansion, and in 1916 the Resler Photo Studio captured this group of enthusiastic and hopeful buyers as they awaited the beginning of a group drawing for lots in Lake Worth (the town south of West Palm Beach, not submerged land in the lake by the same name) and in the Everglades, which, in those days, began barely a mile from downtown, just as it did outside Miami.

The Pioneer Bank, formerly the Dade County Bank. With careful fiscal management and control, it grew along with the new county, and by 1915 was in its new building, awaiting future growth.

This 1918 William N. Miller photograph illustrates changes in bathing attire, as shown by the bare legs of the swimmer at right and diver at left.

Historians owe unending thanks to the early photographers in Miami, Hollywood, Fort Lauderdale, and Fort Pierce, and their contemporaries at the Resler Photo Studio in West Palm Beach, for their stunning imagery and high-grade photo art. Preserving much of Palm Beach County's history on film, Resler even photographed his own studio, shown here on Myrtle Street in a 1917 scene.

The nattily attired gentleman shown here is believed to be early Palm Beach socialite William N. Miller. Photographed in 1918 or '19, Mr. Miller was the picture of Palm Beach sartorial splendor.

"The Coquina"—the name of a famous hotel in Ormond, Florida—was also the name of a houseboat from Massey, Maryland. Photographed by William N. Miller, the houseboat is docked at Palm Beach in 1918.

Although regular visitors to the sands of Miami Beach, these three stunning Miami women made the trek to the Palm Beaches sometime in 1918 or 1919 to bask in the glow of the famous (and infamous) who frequented Palm Beach, well before Miami became the epicenter of Florida's international fame. From left are Joyce Cohen, Myrna Meyers (it was said that Myrna Loy, the famed actress, was named for this Myrna because of her great beauty and serene countenance), and Joyce Schrager.

On the shores of Lake Worth, a golfer practices her drive as she prepares to tee off on the Palm Beach course.

Among the greatest names in Florida—and American—architectural annals is that of Addison Mizner. Usually recognized as the designer and builder of Boca Raton, Mizner was commissioned often to design homes in the Palm Beaches. Included in his Palm Beach portfolio was the home of Charles Munn, which was built in 1919.

The man who built not only Palm Beach and West Palm Beach but much, if not most, of the entire east coast of Florida, the legendary Henry Morrison Flagler (January 2, 1830–May 20, 1913). Starting from modest beginnings, Flagler would eventually become the partner of John D. Rockefeller and one of the founders of the Standard Oil Company. A man many say was the greatest name and person in the history of the Sunshine State, his legendary exploits, achievements, and accomplishments in Florida will forever be the stuff of legend.

A Decade Begins with a Roar
—and Ends with a Limp

(1920–1929)

The end of the First World War was the beginning of a change in Florida unforeseen by even the most insightful. Almost as soon as the war ended, people started pouring into the state, mostly by train but later supplemented by motor coaches (buses) and private automobiles, although a trip of any length was still a rather dicey proposition when driving the state's more primitive roads.

The great Florida real estate boom of the 1920s was not quite as frenzied in Palm Beach as it was in the Miami area, but there was speculation aplenty and land sales took quantum leaps, with prices for property tripling and quadrupling in a single day.

The Florida East Coast Railway, its single track overwhelmed by the huge jump in business, mortgaged itself with the intent of building new shops and yards (including at West Palm Beach), buying all new steam locomotives and equipment, upgrading stations, and double-tracking the entire railroad.

For the 1925–26 season, the FEC operated twelve passenger trains daily through West Palm Beach, several of them continuing to serve the toney island on the other side of Lake Worth. Two of those trains continued past West Palm and Miami to Key West, but the growth of business in the Palm Beaches necessitated a third train, originating in West Palm Beach and terminating in Key West. The "boom" was so massive that the Seaboard Air Line Railway was extended from Wildwood, in North Central Florida, to and through West Palm Beach in order to reach Miami.

The four cataclysmic events of 1926, culminating with the disastrous Miami hurricane of September 17th–18th, were the harbinger of the Great Depression. Business began declining early that year. In 1928, a hurricane of unprecedented proportions blasted ashore at West Palm Beach, ravaged Palm Beach County, and killed hundreds of migrant workers and residents in and around Lake Okeechobee.

The 1920s were both the most vibrant and the most destructive in the county's history. To this day, tales of Palm Beach County's 1920s boom and bust remain ingrained in the minds and history of the region. First-hand accounts are still a staple of education in every college, school, and public library in the county.

Addison Mizner would see his fame grow exponentially, culminating in his creation of Boca Raton and its famous club and hotel of the same name. The street, Via Mizner is named for him. In the early Twenties he designed and was architect for another of the grand Palm Beach homes, this the residence of Arthur B. Claflin at 800 South County Road. There were later additions to the building, although it remained substantially the same.

Gus' Baths were a Palm Beach fixture for years, as those not staying at the ocean-front Breakers Hotel often wished to "take the waters" and enjoy the sand and surf of Palm Beach. The subject of many stories and postcards, Gus' did not hesitate to welcome visitors to "Our Ocean," implying that Gus controlled visitor access to—and enjoyment of—the Atlantic Ocean.

Palm Beach County extends well to the west, encompassing the communities on the east side of Lake Okeechobee as well as South Bay at the "bottom" of the lake. One east-side community, Chosen, was reachable only by poor roads or by boat on the Hillsboro Canal when this photograph was made in 1922. A fishing and farming community, its railway station actually had "Belle Glade" on one side and "Chosen" on the other, the FEC referring to the two communities as one in its timetables.

One of the most vicious gangs of robbers and thugs in the U.S. was the infamous Ashley gang that robbed banks and businesses in Palm Beach County and further north. The outlaws even held up an FEC train. Fortunately for the people of Florida, Sheriff Bob Baker, a steely eyed, no-nonsense lawman, would be instrumental in bringing the desperados to justice.

The western edge of the county is replete with agricultural communities including Belle Glade-Chosen, Canal Point, Pahokee, and South Bay. This photograph from the 1920s shows beans from the Lake Okeechobee growing region being unloaded at the eastern end of the West Palm Beach Canal.

Seaboard Air Line Railway Chairman S. Davies Warfield always bristled at the thought of turning his trains over to the FEC at Jacksonville in order to get them to Miami. With the coming of the great Florida land boom, he ordered construction of a new main line from Central Florida, cutting across the peninsula above Lake Okeechobee and heading on a beeline for West Palm Beach, then turning south for Miami. By 1924 his crews, having reached West Palm, were hard at work extending the railroad down the east coast in direct competition with their former employer.

On March 18, 1925, the second Breakers fire occurred, this one far more damaging than the one of June 1903. The winter season would end within a week, but the hotel was still open, ensuring a fairly large guest count. Following the conflagration, the hotel was rebuilt, and the third Breakers, a marvel of concrete and steel construction, is still thriving today.

As Clematis Street grew in importance, and traffic increased dramatically, parking in the center of the roadway was discontinued, and curbside parking instituted instead. Here, in 1924, with the great Florida boom in full sway and no thoughts that a "bust" was even remotely possible in the near future (it would come beginning in late 1926) a crowd is gathering at the Edward Roody Real Estate office. This view faces west on Clematis from Narcissus Avenue.

The third Breakers would open to grand acclaim, the all-concrete structure no longer a fire hazard. Here, the stunning beauty of the new hotel's lobby lounge is evident. It is still a glamorous destination for travelers from throughout the world today.

The Olive was one of West Palm Beach's early hotels catering primarily to business travelers. Most likely located on Olive Avenue, the hotel is shown in 1925 in a photograph taken by Pownall Studio.

Following Flagler's death, his widow, Mary Lily Kenan Flagler, would marry Judge Robert "Bob" Worth Bingham, later associated for many years with the Louisville *Courier-Journal* newspaper. In 1917, she died under mysterious circumstances. The estate put Whitehall up for sale, and it was eventually purchased by a group that turned it into a hotel of the same name. It did not return to the Flagler heirs until Henry Flagler's granddaughter, Jean Flagler Matthews, purchased the property, formed a foundation, and had the hotel torn down. The home, dedicated to the memory of Henry Flagler, is now a museum bearing his name.

Sometime after the Whitehall estate became a hotel, this photograph of the dining terrace was made. The hotel utilized the main entrance room of the house as its lobby and check-in area, but today no trace of the hotel or its functions remains.

Taken from above Lake Worth in the very early 1920s, this view shows both Whitehall and the Royal Poinciana Hotel, the FEC's entry to Palm Beach to the north of the hotel (at far left in this view). The original bridge was south of Whitehall, but Mrs. Flagler objected to the train noise and her husband simply moved the bridge's location further to the north. The track south of Whitehall remained as the mule-trolley track connecting the two sides of the island.

Looking east across Lake Worth, this late 1920s view shows both the Royal Poinciana (directly in front of the camera) and the Whitehall Hotel at right. The Poinciana would be torn down in the early 1930s, a victim of age and its wooden construction.

Once the Whitehall Hotel opened, the owners, much to their credit, made every effort to maintain a first-class operation. One elegant example, shown here, was the sculpture in the patio of the hotel, maintained with fresh flowers on a daily basis.

By 1925, Clematis had become the principal business street of West Palm Beach and Palm Beach County, thriving in the heart of the Florida boom. Among its stores were Max Sirkin's men's furnishings; Sam Sable, clothier; and the hat store of Joseph Schupler. The Seaboard Railway ticket office is on the left.

By 1926, long-distance telephoning was a way of life. In order to handle the ever-increasing volume of calls thrust upon it by the great boom of the 1920s, Southern Bell installed a brand-new long-distance switchboard in West Palm Beach, responsible for all Palm Beach County long-line calls. At least ten operators are visible in the photo.

While Palm Beach County would be severely battered by the horrible 1928 hurricane, the September 17th–18th, 1926, disaster was no slouch, either. Here, Lake Worth has overflowed the Palm Beach ferry building, and water covers the boulevard facing Palm Beach that would later become West Palm Beach's Flagler Drive.

Another victim of the 1926 hurricane was the sailboat *Marchioness,* stranded over a seawall at Palm Beach. The 1926 storm was one of four disasters that led Florida into the "bust" that was the harbinger of the worldwide Great Depression, which began three years later.

The 1926 storm (this was before hurricanes were named; they were simply known by the dates of landfall) wreaked immeasurable damage on Palm Beach County. Ralph W. Moore, of Wakulla, Florida, was serving as Seaboard Air Line depot ticket agent when the storm hit and is shown here walking around the parking area of the Florida Motor Coach Line garage. Many of the busses were damaged beyond repair.

Shown around 1927, the Northwood Office sign dominates this scene, with McCreary's Drugs at left. The Maddock Building, at right, was home to a number of offices and small stores.

On March 10, 1927, "A. E. Z.," "Chas.," and "Mgr. Rader" are standing in front of Charley's Café, adjacent to the Olive Hotel. It is possible that "Chas." is the Charley of Charley's Café and the two unidentified men second and third from left are the cooks.

Olive Avenue is the cross street shown at the next intersection. That corner, Clematis and Olive, was one of West Palm's busiest. Prominent in this view are the Western Union office and Sable's Shoe Store. For shopping and commerce, Clematis was to West Palm what Flagler Street was to Miami.

Among Palm Beach's most exclusive shopping locales was the Plaza Shops, shown here around 1928. With exclusive stores and residences above, the building was an outstanding Palm Beach landmark for many years.

Another of the Addison Mizner-designed Palm Beach mansions was the home of Dr. Preston Pope Satterwhite at 910 South Ocean Boulevard. The house, named Casa Florencia, included a cathedral-windowed dining room, shown at left.

For many years, passenger trains were allowed on the island of Palm Beach, but automobiles were not. Later, of course, the prohibition ended, but well into the 1940s the pedicabs, almost always driven by an African American, were a Palm Beach staple, and for many, the main mode of transport.

Taken in 1927 by Resler Photo Studio, this fine image is of the Kettler Theater (left) and the Citizen's Bank (right). A Florida coconut palm frond graces the upper left of the photo.

The Everglades Club was one of the most exclusive private clubs in the world; membership was a rare privilege. Its building was designed by architect Addison Mizner. This late 1928 photo was taken prior to the construction of the new wings.

A close-up of the employees of the Palm Beach Bottling Works does not identify any of them except James E. Cook, fifth from left. The man at right is apparently a manager but is not identified in the photo.

The Palm Beach Bottling Works was the home of Nu-Grape and Orange Crush, among other warmly recalled soft drinks. In this image taken by the H. S. Bell Photo Company, the man seventh from left is identified as James E. Cook.

96

Addison Mizner was building his reputation one building at a time, and in 1924, his Worth Avenue Arcade opened, one of the most exclusive and stylish shopping venues in the nation. This photo was shot in 1928 looking east on Worth Avenue.

Palm Beach's Singer Building was on Royal Palm Way. Designed by Mizner and opened in 1925, this building housed offices on the first floor. The upper floors featured apartments arranged around a tiled patio on the second floor.

The Beach Club was an exclusive gaming retreat, presided over by Col. Edward R. Bradley. It was of such high repute that it survived well past the constitutional repeal of games of chance in Florida, and Col. Bradley remains one of the most famous—yet enigmatic—figures in Palm Beach's history.

INTO THE DEPTHS OF DEPRESSION

(1930–1939)

The 1930s opened on a low note. The depression that began with the events of 1926 in South Florida was merely a forerunner of the cataclysm that followed the stock market crash in October 1929 and the subsequent run on banks. Business declined rapidly. The Royal Poinciana closed its doors for good and was torn down in 1932. Train service on the Palm Beach branch was discontinued by the FEC, and with the end of passenger service to the island, the one-mile branch from West Palm Beach was abandoned. An incredible and glorious era in Palm Beach's history was at an end.

As the Great Depression deepened, efforts to assist the citizenry increased. State and local programs were put in place to aid the homeless and hungry. Although there were no Civilian Conservation Corps camps on Palm Beach, there were Works Progress Administration (WPA) projects in Palm Beach County, including the Florida Writers Project, which employed out-of-work writers to record the area's history.

Between Jacksonville and points north, and between West Palm Beach and Miami, the FEC Railway had only seven through trains scheduled during the 1937–38 season. The Seaboard Air Line had just four. Freight business, which had caused the FEC to mortgage itself in 1926, was so sparse that following the great 1935 hurricane, which destroyed forty miles of the railroad's Key West Extension, the company opted not to rebuild, given that only one freight and one passenger train were operating in each direction between Miami and Key West. As the threat of war loomed, however, the military determined the county would be an ideal area for Coast Guard and Naval Air stations from the Jupiter Inlet south.

Even newspapers suffered as advertising declined dramatically, but by 1938 businesses began to see an upturn. That same year, the Seaboard operated its first streamlined, diesel-powered train, followed in 1939 by the Atlantic Coast Line's Florida East Coast Tamiami Champion and the FEC's Jacksonville-Miami Henry M. Flagler. All trains stopped for at least ten minutes at West Palm. By the end of the decade, most trains on both railroads were running full, year-round. Commercial airline service, which had linked Miami with the Northeast beginning in 1931, did not reach the Palm Beaches until 1936. It ended with the beginning of World War II and finally resumed in 1948.

This March 19, 1930, photo shows only a minimal number of people enjoying the shores of Palm Beach County, once packed with winter season visitors. The beaches would remain essentially empty until the Great Depression eased late in the decade.

This woman was photographed March 19, 1930, next to the giant roots of a thirty-eight-year-old bombax ceiba, commonly called a silk cotton tree, red silk tree, and other names. This giant was planted in 1892 on the grounds of the Royal Poinciana Hotel.

The FEC bridge, just visible at the left edge of this 1930 picture, will be gone by 1935. The Royal Poinciana is in the center with the Whitehall Hotel to the south (right) of it. Across the island from the RP is The Breakers, which stands as stately today as it did then.

Even during the height of the Depression, many golfers found the means to continue playing. Pictured here, just prior to tee off, are noted Palm Beach duffers William F. Kenny, M. Tennes, Lewis Smith and Edwin M. John.

Through the Federal Emergency Relief Administration (FERA), communities across America received federal assistance during the Depression. The West Palm Beach area received funds to provide nursery services for children of all races, including the boys and girls photographed here, May 6, 1935.

Another Palm Beach County FERA project was assistance in building Morrison Field, an airport which opened in December 1936. In World War II, it would become an Army Air Force base. Following the war, on August 11, 1948, Morrison Field became Palm Beach International Airport. Construction work was in its early stages when this photo was taken on May 3, 1935.

A crew was photographed April 30, 1935, constructing the Sherman Point drawbridge, one of the local opportunities created by FERA's efforts to provide out-of-work Americans with employment.

On May 6, 1935, a FERA photographer snapped this picture of a group of women in a West Palm Beach factory, learning how to prepare a mattress for shipping. Note the sewing machines then in vogue, in the foreground.

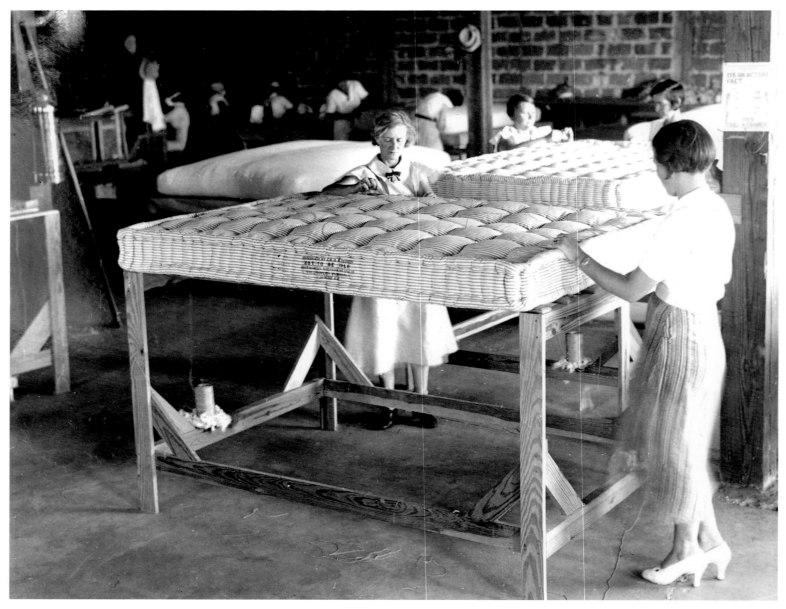

In a close-up view, several women are completing the mattress-building task and going through the final quality-control steps prior to boxing the finished product.

As part of its mission to create jobs, FERA assisted cities and towns with community enrichment projects. The West Palm Beach parks and recreation department showed off its new City Park open-air auditorium, complete with band shell and facilities, shortly after completion. This photo was made May 2, 1935.

Through a photography project, FERA and other government agencies attempted to document life in America. Taken in 1935, the photo was made at Green Acres Nursery School in WPB. The children, for the most part, appear oblivious to the fact that their see-saw ride was being recorded for posterity.

Programs for children's dental health did not become widespread in America until the 1930s. This view of nine adorable tykes was made at Green Acres Nursery School, May 2, 1935.

West Palm Beach High School maintains a proud tradition as a great educational facility in Palm Beach County, and generations of Palm Beachites are proud to have been "Wildcats." Even in 1935, the school was having growing pains. This April 30 FERA image recorded a new addition as it neared completion.

On May 1, 1935, local school children enjoyed the day with games and entertainment at West Palm Beach's Phipps Park.

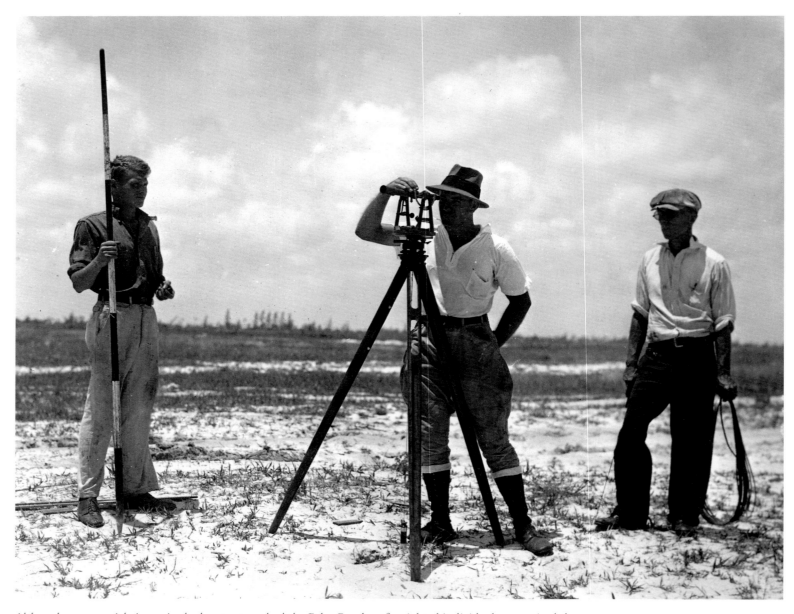

Although commercial air service had not yet reached the Palm Beaches, far-sighted individuals recognized that the day would soon be at hand. On May 3, 1935, this surveying team was laying groundwork for the eventual building of what would, in 1948, become Palm Beach International Airport.

Colonel Edward R. Bradley owned and operated the beach club and casino at Palm Beach. The elegance and glamour of the club were a match for the swankiest of gaming emporiums anywhere in America or Europe, and it remained in business long after gaming was constitutionally outlawed in Florida. Bradley's was for many years a Palm Beach landmark.

The Seaboard Railway began diesel-electric, streamlined passenger train service from Penn Station, New York, to Miami a full year ahead of its great competitors, the Atlantic Coast Line-Florida East Coast Railway combination. The companies dueled endlessly for the New York-to-Florida passenger business. In December 1938, just prior to the beginning of service, the Seaboard exhibited its new locomotives and streamliner equipment. The platform with West Palm Beach's station name appears just to the right of the nose of the diesel.

A Sleeping Giant Begins to Awaken

(1940–1949)

The decade of the 1940s, decidedly differently than the previous one, began with not only a feeling of hope, but with a belief that the worst depression in history was coming to an end. Unhappily, though, the threat that foreign wars might expand to include America loomed like a thunderhead on the horizon.

Streamliner service on the FEC-ACL and Seaboard operated through Palm Beach County daily, with the FEC's line coming south along the east coast from Jacksonville, the Seaboard's coming east from central Florida. West Palm Beach was the Seaboard's first Palm Beach County passenger stop southbound and its last northbound. Streamlined trains vastly increased the number of visitors to the county, and both railroads added stops south of Palm Beach as the region grew.

Automobile traffic was also increasing by leaps and bounds, but that came to a jarring halt following the December 7, 1941, Japanese attack on Pearl Harbor. Gasoline rationing cut civilian automobile travel back drastically, and auto-makers ceased production of civilian models to concentrate all resources on the war effort.

Though Palm Beach County was not a major military center, the number of Army Air Force, Navy, and Coast Guard people who journeyed north from Miami and Fort Lauderdale to see the Palm Beaches increased dramatically. Military personnel assigned to Camp Murphy just south of Hobe Sound, to Morrison Field in West Palm Beach, and to Camp Griffith at Boca Raton proved a blessing for merchants.

The Royal Poinciana had been torn down in 1932, but The Breakers continued to operate, though much of its capacity, like that of the other large Palm Beach and West Palm Beach Hotels, was taken up by wartime service personnel.

When hostilities ended in 1945, changes came quickly, and the county adapted almost immediately to a peace-time economy. National advertising campaigns in coordination with hotels, railroads and, finally, Eastern Air Lines, convinced war-weary travelers to spend their dollars in the Palm Beaches.

Growth continued slowly at first, the area being overshadowed by Greater Miami as Miami and Miami Beach began their postwar boom, but the groundwork was being laid and seeds sown for a later growth spurt that would eventually change the face of Palm Beach County.

Lake Worth looks calm in this 1941 Charles Foster photograph of the Palm Beach Biltmore, but storm clouds in Europe and Asia are about to envelop America.

On January 13, 1941, the SS *Manhattan,* a 24,000-ton luxury liner of the United States Lines, sailing perilously close to the Florida mainland, suddenly ran aground three hundred yards off the coast, nine miles north of Palm Beach. After sitting helplessly for twenty-two days, she was finally freed by the Coast Guard Cutter *Mojave* on February 4, 1941. The *Manhattan,* rechristened *Wakefield,* became a troop transport vessel in World War II.

Photographs of Colonel Edward R. Bradley are rare. He was a horseman who owned Idle Hour Farm in Lexington, Kentucky, and, of course, he was the proprietor of Bradley's Beach Club. Shown here in 1943 with his Afromobile driver, he appears quite relaxed as he takes a break from the rigors of hospitality management.

The Styx had changed dramatically from its previous incarnation by the time this photograph was made by Resler Photo Studio in 1941.

In 1946, Elsie Anderson and Florence Lainhart, two Palm Beach beauties, posed for a cheesecake-style photo. The image, captured by a Florida Department of Commerce photographer at West Palm Beach, was intended for use in State of Florida publicity campaigns.

Elegant, high-quality browsing and buying have long been the order of the day on Worth Avenue or any other shopping street in Palm Beach. The cars, palm trees, and beautiful buildings tell the story of one of America's most desirable destinations.

The Florida Department of Commerce was, for many years, responsible for Florida's tourism and business promotion and never missed an opportunity to glamorize every part of the state. The beauty of Palm Beach was perfect for these publicity gambits. The private yacht *Southward-Ho* was used often to show people enjoying the Intracoastal Waterway and Lake Worth.

Even the banks on Palm Beach bespoke elegance and refinement. In 1946, it was important to show stability and safety, with the memory of the Depression still fresh in the public mind.

Although not quite like today's "drive-through banking," the First National Bank of Palm Beach arranged to open a window so that patrons would not have to actually come into the bank, although they did have to exit their cars. As this 1946 photograph shows, customers could "ring bell for service" at the Auto Teller window.

West Palm, across Lake Worth from Palm Beach in 1946, looks very much like the famous view of Miami across Biscayne Bay from Watson Island, proving the Palm Beaches could convey the same stunning "big city" image.

The Beach Boys may have memorized California girls in their songs, but Florida's beaches have never lacked for beauties either, whether natives or tourists. Here, famed Palm Beach photographer Dean Cornwell photographs Mrs. Hjordis Termesden, a Swedish visitor, in 1947.

Bethesda-by-the-Sea Episcopal Church is one of Palm Beach's oldest and most beautiful houses of worship. The bell tower shown here is one of Palm Beach's most recognizable landmarks.

Edward T. Stotesbury was a famed Philadelphia industrialist who died at the age of 89 in 1938. His widow, Eva R. Stotesbury, moved to their Palm Beach home, "El Mirasol," and following her death in 1946, the entire contents of El Mirasol were sold between February 25 and March 3, 1947, one of the greatest "house sales" in the history of Palm Beach County. Admission to the auction was $2.00, a sum—at the time—guaranteed to keep the less desirable away.

Among the items placed for sale at the El Mirasol auction were the estate's vehicles. At least six of them (and possibly more) were sold during the seven-day event.

A portion of the crowd at the Stotesbury auction is visible here. Note that all of the men are in ties and jackets and that most of the women are wearing the chapeaus of the day.

Three strong men were
required to cart away this
heavy piece of furniture
purchased at the El Mirasol
extravaganza.

Worth Avenue, on Palm Beach, was and is one of the most glamorous shopping streets in America. With most of the stores and restaurants now open year-round, it is a busy and active destination, frequented by tourists and residents alike. For many years, shoppers from as far south as Key West and as far north as Daytona would make the trip to Palm Beach a grand, one-day excursion.

The 1947 hurricane was another of the bruisers that severely affected Palm Beach County, causing millions of dollars in damage and, due to farmland flooding, retarding agricultural production for months. The huge, Category 4 storm with sustained winds of more than 120 miles per hour, came ashore September 17th near Hillsboro Inlet, but the rains were so intense and so sustained that much of the area from north Palm Beach to Pompano Beach in Broward County was flooded.

Locating an image that includes the name of a Palm Beach pedicab, or Afromobile, driver is a rare, memorable, and highly rewarding find. Pedalling the beautiful Elizabeth Harvel during the 1947 winter season is long-time pedicab professional Homer Bacon Smith. His service was often requested by those who appreciated his gracious demeanor and personal attention, as well as his fine sense of humor.

Yale crew members took time off to pose with Florida governor Millard Caldwell's daughters, Sue (left) and Sally (right). Seated from left are John Lawrence, Dick Olmsted, Bill Meyer, John Kingsbury, and Greg Gates. The two men kneeling at left are Don Cadle and Bob Perew. Standing are crew members Pete Peacock, George Carver, Jimmy Beggs, Stew Griffing, and Sty Lawn. The photograph was made on the grounds of the Everglades Club during the 1948 rowing regatta. It is likely the crew was feted there sometime during their stay.

Lake Worth was a spectacular setting for winter crew competition. Many northern schools' athletes were delighted beyond words to spend part of the winter in the glorious climate and surroundings of the Palm Beaches. On January 2, 1948 (coincidentally, the 118th anniversary of Henry Flagler's birth), Ivy League rivals Yale University and the University of Pennsylvania are matching stroke for stroke in this scene from one of their numerous rowing regatta matches.

141

It is extremely rare to see public transit in a Palm Beach photo, hence this 1947 picture is a bus collector's gem as well as a true P. B. "find." This picture taken on County Road of one of the Palm Beach transit line's late-1930s White or Ford buses is one of the few known images of them.

In the early 1940s the area in and near Boynton Beach was primarily farm land. At the Flatwoods Plantation, pineapples were still grown, although by the end of World War II all cultivation of that plant here would cease. Farm foreman W. E. Roush, left, talks with county agricultural agent M. U. Mounts, who is holding a golden pineapple.

The war had ended, and America was returning to normal in 1947. Famed artists Arthur William Brown (left) (1881–1966) and Russell Patterson (1896–1977) were photographed sketching Florence Kallender at the Coral Beach Club.

A 1946 view of Worth Avenue brings back memories of long-time retailers. Close to the camera is the Ted Stone wine and liquor store, popular with P. B. socialites. Next to it is the famous restaurant Ta-boo. Both have been gone for many years.

Ripley's junk, the *Mon Lei,* was often seen in Lake Worth and is shown here at one of the private piers. Robert
Ripley of "Believe it or Not" fame purchased the junk in 1946. Its name means "infinity."

Pictured aboard the "Mon Lei" are Robert Ripley, his secretary Lisa Wisse, and his dog, Schlimiel. The photo was taken in 1947 in the junk's alcove.

Following the September 2nd, 1935, hurricane, the FEC abandoned the Key West Extension and moved the car ferry operation to Port Everglades. With the coming of World War II, the government took over the car ferries "for the duration." Following the war, the FEC sold the operation to the West India Fruit and Steamship Company, which moved it to the Port of Palm Beach at Riviera Beach. This late-1940s aerial view shows two of the car ferries at the port and a full complement of freight cars awaiting loading for the trip to Cuba.

By the late 1940s, fashion designers were using Palm Beach as a backdrop for the introduction of their newest designs. In 1948, at the Palm Beach Biltmore, Lily Dache introduced her newest creations. From left, model Joan Johnson, C. L. Larsen, Jean Depres (Ms. Dache's husband), and model Euvera Benway enjoy the Florida sun as well as the gala event. Mr. Depres was, at the time, an executive with fragrance manufacturer Coty Company.

In January 1948, the National Association of Chain Drug Stores held their yearly convention in Palm Beach. Among the celebrities in attendance was the then-famous, forty-seven-inch tall "Johnny" (Johnny Roventini, 1912–1998) who was known for his highly starched bellhop uniform complete with pillbox hat and his stentorian "Call for Philll-lip Mohrrr-is!" cry. His national recognition reached such heights that he was hired to pull prize-winning tickets during the convention raffle, the gifts ranging from radios to boxes of fresh Florida fruit.

By 1946, when this photo was taken, West Palm Beach was the second-most important business center of South Florida and the Gold Coast, with only Miami having a larger and busier downtown. The city center would soon house a Burdine's department store as well as other well-known, high-volume retail outlets. This view is nothing if not pure nostalgia, for today not a single building shown still exists.

Thanks to this marvelous photograph, we KNOW where Joe Dimaggio had gone to in January of 1948! On the thirteenth of that month, the famous "Yankee Clipper" was in West Palm Beach for "R 'n R," and that morning he made his way to Bill McGowan's Umpire School to visit with friends. Shortly after arrival, he encountered three-year-old Larry Valencourt and took the time to show little Larry how to hold the bat.

On January 10, 1948, FEC 4-8-2-type steam locomotive Number 813 carried convention attendees to West Palm Beach aboard an excursion train, "The National Association of Chain Drug Stores (NACDS) Special." It is uncertain who took this photograph, but possibly it was long-time FEC Railway company photographer Harry M. Wolfe.

Still bundled in their winter finery, which they would soon shed, Mr. and Mrs. W. S. Marshall, of Cleveland, Ohio, detrain from the NACDS Special. The Marshalls, representing Cunningham Drug Co. of Detroit, would later remark that they were unprepared for both the beauty of the surroundings and the hospitality that they encountered during the convention, and that they would return to Florida as soon as practicable.

The Breakers is the last of the Flagler System Hotels and remains an American icon. Photographed in 1949, this is the south tower of the front entrance of the hotel. Although minor changes have been made, the front remains very much the same today, the view recognizable immediately to anyone approaching the hotel from the west side.

Florence Lainhart of West Palm Beach became Florida's "Year Round Girl of 1947" and was seen nationally in the state's promotional advertising. The image of Florida as a winter-season-only resort was being discarded by hoteliers and business people who recognized that visitors could and would come to the sunshine state throughout the year.

Ray Bolger, best known for his portrayal of the Scarecrow in *The Wizard of Oz,* was an accomplished song-and-dance man. For the National Association of Chain Drug Stores' 1948 convention, Bolger was the headliner, shown here in the midst of a January thirteenth performance, following which he received a standing ovation.

In 1948, former Jacksonville city council member Fuller Warren (1905–1973) was elected governor of Florida and was inaugurated in January 1949. On January 5, well-known Florida photographer Forrest Granger snapped this view of the Palm Beach County inaugural parade float, the self-propelled "boat" *Miss Lake Park,* complete with a bevy of stunning, bathing-suit-attired beauties.

CHANGE IS IN THE AIR

(1950–1959)

The 1950s would see dramatic changes as new inventions such as television, reliable room air conditioners, transistor radios, and Hula Hoops became popular. Rock 'n' roll became the anthem of the teen generation. By mid-decade, half the young men in America wanted to have hair like Elvis Presley, and more than half the young women swooned over him.

Road building went into full swing with improvements in Palm Beach County on U.S. 98, U.S. 27, U.S. 441, U.S. 1, and many county and local streets and highways. Airline service expanded at West Palm Beach's airport, with Mackey Airlines, Bahamas Air, and "Q" Airways joining Eastern.

Florida East Coast and Seaboard passenger train services remained strong. The FEC's ticket office at 23 Datura Street in downtown West Palm stayed busy throughout the decade.

The Fifties also saw a surge in growth in the county. Palm Beach Shores was incorporated in 1951, North Palm Beach in 1956, and Palm Beach Gardens in 1959. Highland Beach had incorporated in 1949, and oceanfront land in that community was selling for $125 a foot in 1950. Today it fetches $80,000 per front foot!

The influx of new residents put a strain on the schools, and new facilities opened throughout the county. Palm Beach Community College, which opened in 1933 as one of Florida's first community colleges, was revitalized in 1955 when the county commission gave the school 114 acres in Lake Worth. For the first time, the college had its own campus. Previously, it held classes in various secondary-school and municipal buildings throughout the county, including some at the old Morrison Army Air Field. The state legislature also gave the school over a million dollars for new buildings, and in 1956 classes began on the Lake Worth campus.

In 1959 Perry Publications purchased the *Delray Journal* and combined the *Journal* and *News* to form the *Delray Beach News Journal*. By the end of the decade, changes in thinking, dress, attitudes, and politics had taken place, forerunners of the social upheaval that would occur in the 1960s.

In 1936, Claude D. Pepper (1900–1989) was elected to the U.S. Senate, where he would remain until defeated in 1950 by George Smathers. The 1950 campaign was particularly vicious. According to legend, Smathers accused Pepper of being an extrovert and having a sister who was a thespian, assuming rural voters wouldn't know the meaning of his words, but the story was probably a hoax. When Pepper's advertising Jeep was involved in a collision, Smathers' friend, Carl L. Hahn, sent Smathers this picture with a note that said, "Here's what is left of the Pepper machine in Palm Beach County!" Some years later, Pepper was elected to the U.S. Congress, representing a Dade County district.

In 1951, the Florida State Chamber of Commerce held its thirty-fifth annual meeting in West Palm Beach. The keynote speaker was Florida governor Fuller Warren, shown here at the microphone. To his left is Florida's senior U. S. Senator Spessard L. Holland.

The groundbreaking for Temple Israel in West Palm Beach in 1951 was "groundbreaking," indeed. The Palm Beach County Jewish community had always taken a back seat to that of Miami, so building a new temple was a major achievement for the Palm Beaches. Shown speaking is Norman Mirsky. From left are Rabbi Richard Singer, Harry Halpern, Philip Blicher, Alfred Fink, an unidentified man, Alice Gordon, O. P. Gruner, Louis Leibouit, another unidentified attendee, Leon Goldsmith, Mayor Jack Faircloth, and David Tisnower.

The majestic Jupiter Inlet Lighthouse remains active today. First lit on July 10, 1860, it is the oldest existing structure in Palm Beach County. During World War II, it was dimmed with a low-wattage bulb. Several ships were sunk offshore by Nazi submarines, and the sad duty of recovering bodies as they washed ashore fell to the lighthouse keepers. In 1959, the two-story lighthouse keeper's dwelling was torn down and new quarters were built. The lighthouse itself is a national historic landmark.

Glamour photography remained a mainstay of publicity and promotion for the state, particularly for its oceanfront and gulf coast areas.

Palm Beach County, in a major convention coup, hosted the Inter-American Tourism Conference, October 13–15, 1954, featuring events in both West Palm Beach and Palm Beach. Many attendees stayed at the Colony Hotel on Palm Beach. Here, participants enjoy the closing banquet in the hotel's famed dining room.

Growth brings infrastructure improvements. This 1954 photograph shows construction on Florida Power and Light's new generating plant at Riviera Beach was well underway.

Ever since the arrival of Henry Flagler's railroad and hotels, the Palm Beaches have been a magnet for the rich and famous, a stomping ground for politicians and celebrities. Participating in a celebrity golf tournament in the late 1950s, Florida's U.S. Senator George Smathers, at far left, is joined by the Duke of Windsor, who is holding a hat. The man to the right of the duke is believed to be the great "Slammin' Sammy" Snead, who loved Palm Beach and played here almost every winter throughout the 1950s. The man at far right is unidentified and may be a tournament official.

The First Church of Christ, Scientist, at 138 Lakeview Avenue in West Palm, is a stately edifice which has been an area landmark for many years. Though the flora is different, the beautiful building remains as striking as ever.

Lee Petty (1914–2000), a NASCAR pioneer and the father of Richard Petty, drove in his first stock-car race at the age of 35 and in 1959 won the inaugural Daytona 500. In 1953, thirty-nine years old, he is photographed in West Palm Beach with his Dodge, #42.

Fifteen miles west of Palm Beach the Palm Beach-Loxahatchee Company packing house was the destination for Indian River citrus fruits, sent there for shipping throughout the country.

The Plantation Dining Room of The Famous Restaurant was a long-time gathering spot for Lake Worth's residents. Located at 912 Second Avenue North, the restaurant was known for both its food and excellent service.

In the mid-1950s, construction began on Florida's first turnpike, the 110-mile Miami–Ft. Pierce Sunshine State Parkway, which opened in 1957. West Palm Beach was a major interchange and toll collection facility. In addition, a service plaza was built there. This 1956 image shows paving of the southbound roadway is in progress north of the WPB interchange. The northbound lanes had already been paved.

Stately and elegant, the Colony Hotel was opened in 1947. Built in the modified colonial style, it currently has ninety-two recently renovated and updated guest rooms and is a favored dining and dancing spot in the Palm Beaches. Shown here in 1955, the hotel has maintained a reputation for staff excellence and fine service.

Unlike much of Florida, where the view of the ocean or the gulf has been blocked by high rises and private beaches, Palm Beach maintains a policy of keeping the east side of its oceanfront drive open, just as it was in this 1956 Charles Barron photograph.

In the mid-1950s, when the Mass home was built on Everglades Island in Palm Beach County, it was not just modernistic, it was futuristic! A stunning piece of architecture in the style of Frank Lloyd Wright's work, the Mass house is shown here in 1956 in a photograph by Charles Barron.

When the Pratt & Whitney aircraft engine plant opened in 1958, eighteen miles northwest of West Palm Beach on State Road 710—the Bee Line Highway—it was a major economic shot in the arm for the county, providing hundreds of jobs with millions of dollars in annual payrolls. This photo of the employees relaxing at lunch hour in the open-air courtyard was made in 1959.

Completed in 1957, the original Florida Turnpike (the Sunshine State Parkway) extended from Fort Pierce to Miami, with service and facilities plazas at Pompano, West Palm Beach, and Fort Pierce. The newly opened West Palm Beach Service Plaza is shown here in 1958. Francis P. Johnson, who did much of the Turnpike Authority's photo work, made this image.

An Aura of Greatness Emerges

(1960–1967)

The times, they were, indeed, a-changin', as folksinger Bob Dylan famously proclaimed. Some in the county would find those changes unpleasant, uncomfortable, and at times, unpalatable, but Palm Beach County would, nonetheless, be dragged into the late twentieth century, often kicking and screaming.

In 1964, Southeast Florida's first public university, Florida Atlantic, also known as FAU, opened its doors as the first university in the nation to offer only upper-division and graduate level courses. From its initial enrollment of 867, it has grown to house today's student population of 26,000, drawn from all over the world. While the original and main campus remain in Boca Raton, the school now offers courses and programs throughout South Florida, from Fort Pierce and Port St. Lucie in St. Lucie County through Dania Beach, Davie, and Fort Lauderdale in Broward County, with a north Palm Beach County campus in Jupiter.

In 1969, Cox Enterprises purchased most of the newspapers in Palm Beach County, forming Palm Beach Newspapers. James M. Cox, Jr., and the *Palm Beach Post* have endowed a professorship at the University of Florida in new media journalism.

During the 1960s, change came unrelentingly. Two defining moments were the murder of President John F. Kennedy in November 1963 and the passage of the Civil Rights Act by Congress in 1964.

President Kennedy was a frequent visitor to Palm Beach County, where his family maintained a beautiful home on Palm Beach. During his term, the house was guarded around the clock by the Secret Service and was the site of many presidential conferences and meetings. Hundreds of Palm Beachites motorcaded to Miami to welcome the president when he arrived at Miami International Airport just one week before his death.

The Civil Rights Act of 1964 was especially meaningful in Palm Beach County. Many hotels, restaurants, and clubs still followed the state's segregation laws and refused to admit black patrons. In addition, several Palm Beach hotels adhered to the discriminatory practice of "restricted clientele," refusing guest rooms to people known to be of the Jewish faith.

The Anti-Defamation League of B'nai B'rith chose The Breakers for a test case of the Civil Rights Act. In early 1965, a Jewish couple attempting to register at the hotel was told—with news media present—that the hotel "does not accept as guests persons of the Hebrew faith." A lawsuit thus followed that enabled the Supreme Court to vote 9–0 to uphold the Civil Rights Act, forbidding discrimination in America based on race or religion.

Palm Beach County today is a modern, forward-looking center of education, technology, the arts, entertainment, and recreation. It is home to several colleges and universities, great theater venues such as the Kravitz Center, superb art galleries including the Norton, and marvelous history-research facilities, such as the Historical Society of Palm Beach County, Boynton Beach Historical Society, Boca Raton Historical Society, Delray Beach Historical Society, the Henry M. Flagler Museum at Whitehall, and others.

From Jupiter and Tequesta on the north, to Boca Raton on the south, and west to the Lake Okeechobee-anchored towns of Belle Glade, Pahokee, Canal Point, and South Bay, the entire county is repositioning itself for the twenty-first century. Many of the communities are completely redeveloping and upgrading their downtowns, preserving their history while reaching out to a new generation of diners, theatergoers, and entertainment aficionados, presenting opportunities that will help Palm Beach County remain one of the leading destinations of South Florida and the world.

The Brazilian Court opened for business on New Years Day 1926 and became an instant "in-spot" for Palm Beachites and visitors alike. Located just off of Worth Avenue, the hotel currently has eighty rooms and a reputation for fine food and attentive service. In 1960, Palm Beach photographer Francis Johnson recorded one of the hotel's chefs presenting the tomato preparations of several famous chefs, with the beautiful background of the hotel dining room complementing the scene.

Built in 1901 by Henry Flagler for his third wife, Mary Lily (Kenan) Flagler, Whitehall was the couple's primary residence until his death in 1913. Later sold by the Flagler heirs, the home was turned into a luxury hotel with a tower built behind it. In 1959, upon learning that plans were in the works to raze the home, Flagler's granddaughter, Jean Flagler Mathews, formed a foundation and acquired the property, subsequently tearing down the hotel tower. In 1960, Whitehall was opened to the public as the Henry M. Flagler Museum.

Florida's only governor with a Harvard University law degree, Farris Bryant was elected in 1960. In this West Palm Beach photo, Bryant is at left, shaking hands with a constituent. Accompanying him, left to right, are Richard W. Ervin, Edwin L. Mason, Thomas D. Bailey, Ray E. Green, and J. Edwin Larson.

In 1962, Charles Barron photographed a group that went a-fishin' in the Atlantic off the coast of Palm Beach County in hopes of luring the elusive kingfish to their hooks.

In June 1962, photographer Charles Barron focused his lens on the new West Palm Beach Public Library, a facility much needed and long overdue at the time. Now one of Florida's largest and most modern libraries, in the 1960s, the fight to modernize and bring the library system up to date was a difficult struggle.

Three anglers proudly display their catch, a small sailfish, for the camera. This is another of the Charles Barron photos, taken in November 1961.

A leading Florida employer, the Clewiston-based United States Sugar Company owns and operates several mills. One of them was for many years at Bryant, near Canal Point in western Palm Beach County. Shown here around 1962, one of the switch engines is hard at work shifting sugar cane cars before moving them to the mill for processing.

Whitehall's restored ceiling mural, decorations, and painting were strikingly captured by Charles Barron in February 1962.

As with most cities of note, West Palm Beach boasts an active and enthusiastic Chamber of Commerce, known today as the Chamber of Commerce of the Palm Beaches. This Barron photograph shows the Chamber building at 401 Flagler Drive in all its 1965 glory.

Medley's Gifts was, as their advertising stated, "A Very Different Gift Store." Filled with unique and unusual items, the shop at 787 Northlake Boulevard in North Palm Beach was a popular place, but as greater Palm Beach grew, new, even more unusual stores opened, and Medley's went out of business.

This 1965 exterior view of the Pratt & Whitney plant gives an idea of the size of this major Palm Beach County employer. At the time it was constructed, the building shown was P & W's Florida Research and Development Center.

Walking past The Lullabye Shop on Worth Avenue in 1967, Madelyn Bergman and her pooch, Lily, are enjoying the sun, surroundings, and serenity of one of America's most famous shopping streets, as the season comes to a close. In a few days, the stores would be shuttered for the summer.

The Lullabye Shop on Worth Avenue was a favorite for the grandparents and parents of younger children. The store's up-to-date fashions were among the finest selections available in the Palm Beaches. The shop is shown in the Florida sunlight in 1967, with a Jaguar XKE parked in front.

When Claude Kirk, left, took office on January 3, 1967, he became the first Republican governor of Florida in ninety years. In the first year of his 1967–71 term, he married Erika Mattfeld at West Palm Beach. Among the wedding guests was none other than Richard M. Nixon, right, who would become America's president the following year.

Assigned for several years by the Florida East Coast Railway to switching duties in the Palm Beaches, SW1200-type diesel switch engine 229 reposes between shunting moves, its FEC emblem showing proudly toward the front of the locomotive.

Notes on the Photographs

These notes, listed by page number, attempt to include all aspects known of the photographs. Each of the photographs is identified by the page number, photograph's title or description, photographer and collection, archive, and call or box number when applicable. Although every attempt was made to collect all available data, in some cases complete data was unavailable due to the age and condition of some of the photographs and records.